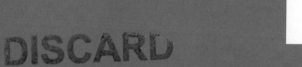

JESSE JACKSON

and Political Power

by Teresa Celsi

Gateway Civil Rights
The Millbrook Press
Brookfield, Connecticut

Interior Design: Tilman Reitzle

Photographs courtesy of: Steele Collection: cover; National Rainbow Coalition: cover inset; AP/Wide World Photos: 1, 14, 15, 18, 19, 22, 23, 24, 27, 30; Schomburg Center for Research in Black Culture: 2-3, 9, 17; Joey Ivansco: 4; The Bettmann Archive: 11, 13, 26; Robert Sengstacke: 20; Cleveland Plain Dealer: 29.

Cataloging-in-Publication Data

Celsi, Teresa
Jesse Jackson and political power.

32 pp.; ill.: (Gateway Civil Rights)
Bibliography: p.
Includes index.

Summary: Jesse Jackson is a black civil rights activist, political leader, and Baptist minister. He has focused attention on the problems of racial discrimination, economic injustice, drug abuse, and teenage pregnancy. He was a candidate for the Democratic presidential nomination in 1984 and 1988.
1. Jackson, Jesse Louis, 1941- 2. Civil Rights.
3. United States–race relations.
1991 B (92) Jackson
ISBN 1-56294-040-6

In the 1960s, blacks were often arrested for demanding an end to segregation.

Jesse Jackson '88

Nineteen eighty-eight was a presidential election year. In Michigan, the Democratic party primary was held on Saturday, March 26. On that day, Democrats in Michigan voted for the man they wanted their party to nominate for president. Most of the experts thought Governor Michael Dukakis of Massachusetts would win.

Also in the race was the Reverend Jesse Jackson. Jackson was a black minister from Chicago and a civil rights leader. The experts thought that white Americans were not ready to elect a black man to be president, so they did not think Jackson had much of a chance to win.

In Michigan, however, Jackson proved that people's expectations were wrong. In the black communities of Detroit and Flint, he won local districts by huge margins. But he also did well in mostly white cities such as Lansing and Kalamazoo. Jackson won a convincing victory in Michigan, astounding the experts.

All his life, Jesse Jackson had worked to prove that people's expectations about him were wrong. He knew that he could do more and be better. The victory in Michigan was a great personal achievement. But it also proved that a black man could win white votes, and maybe even become president.

Jesse Jackson made history at the 1988 Democratic National Convention in Atlanta, Georgia.

"Jesse Ain't Got No Daddy!"

On October 8, 1941, a 16-year-old girl named Helen Burns gave birth to a boy in Greenville, South Carolina. She named him Jesse Louis. But she did not give him his father's last name because she was not married at the time. Jesse's father, a man named Noah Robinson, lived next door, but he was already married to another woman.

Jesse's birth was a scandal in the neighborhood. Helen had to quit school to raise the child, and her church refused to open its doors to her until she apologized to the congregation for her behavior.

Things were difficult for Jesse, too. Other children in the neighborhood picked on him because his mother was not married. They would yell at him: "Jesse ain't got no Daddy! Jesse ain't got no Daddy!"

It hurt to be teased, but Jesse tried not to let it show. He told himself that the bad things happening to him would only make him stronger one day. He knew that if he kept believing in himself he could be somebody special.

Jesse received a lot of help along the way from his grandmother, Mathilda Burns, whom he called Aunt Tibby. "For God's sake, Jesse," Aunt Tibby would say, "promise me you'll be somebody. Nothing is impossible for those who have the Lord. Come hell or high water, if you got the guts, boy, ain't nothing or nobody can turn you around."

Jesse listened to his grandmother and took comfort in God. He and his family attended church regularly. So did most of their neighbors. In fact, throughout the South, many blacks looked to local churches for the strength to endure their many hardships. Churches were places that drew blacks together for a peaceful time away from the white people who had once enslaved them. Churches were also centers of social organization in the black community, and many ministers were political leaders, too.

When Jesse was 9 years old, his mother married a postal worker named Charles Henry Jackson. Jesse finally got a daddy. From the beginning, Jackson treated Jesse as his own son. He legally adopted Jesse and gave him the last name of Jackson.

Jesse was fortunate because the Jacksons lived in a house that was comfortable by Greenville standards. It had both electricity and indoor toilets. Many blacks in Greenville had to live without these things.

Most blacks lived in "shotgun" houses. These were single-story buildings divided by thin walls into two or three rooms. The front door would open on a living room. Across the living room would be a door to the bedroom, and across the bedroom would be a door to the kitchen.

They were called shotgun houses because a bullet shot through the front door would travel straight through the house and out the back door. During the 1940s and 1950s, when Jesse was growing up, many shotgun houses in Greenville had no indoor plumbing, and some had no electricity at all. Instead, they were heated by wood or coal stoves and lit up at night by candles and lanterns.

Many of the shotgun houses in Jesse's neighborhood were owned by a white man named Mr. Helum. On Saturdays, he would drive up in his truck to collect the rent. Many of his tenants, however, were too poor to pay. They hid out in the bushes when he came because they were afraid he would throw them out. Then they would have no place at all to live. "He'd be chasing them to collect," Jesse recalled years later. "They were filled with fear, and I resented that."

Jesse learned very early on that being black meant being picked on by white people. In the South during that time, almost all public places were segregated, which meant that blacks were kept apart from whites. Blacks could not drink from white-only water fountains. They could not eat at white-only lunch counters or watch movies in white-only theaters. Whites also kept the best jobs and the best schools for themselves.

Once, when Jesse was 8 years old, he and some friends went into a store to buy some candy. The man behind the counter was white. Jesse whistled to get his attention. Whites whistled at blacks all the time. But for blacks to do the same thing was an entirely different matter in the segregated South. When the man behind the counter saw that Jesse was black, he pulled out a gun and pointed it right at Jesse. "Goddamn you!" the man said. "Don't you ever whistle at a white man again!" Jesse ran all the way home from the store, trembling with fear and rage.

Another time, Jesse and his friends were outside a cigar store listening to a boxing match on the radio. The black heavyweight champion Joe Louis was fighting a white contender. "Joe Louis was battering the guy without mercy," Jesse remembered. "But we didn't dare show any emotion over a black man beating a white one. We knew it would anger the white shopkeeper and his friends."

This sign was one of many examples of racism in the Old South.

Becoming Somebody

From the time he was young, Jesse was not happy unless he was the best at whatever he was doing. In elementary school, his teachers said he was a "cut-up" because he fooled around too much. But Jesse soon straightened out in high school.

One of his sixth-grade teachers said, "I used to tell him that the only chance he had to be somebody was to learn while it was easy—while he was young and had nothing else to do but learn."

In the ninth grade, Jesse was elected president of his class at Sterling High, and later he became president of the honor society. He was also good at sports. His high school coach said he had never worked with as talented a quarterback as Jesse.

After his graduation from Sterling in 1959, Jesse got an offer to play professional baseball. Instead, he went to the University of Illinois on a football scholarship. But the coaches at Illinois would not let him play quarterback. They believed that only a white person was capable of playing well in that crucial leadership position.

Jesse was furious. He left Illinois after just one year, and transferred to the all-black North Carolina Agricultural and Technical College in Greensboro. There he got to play quarterback.

Football, however, was not the only reason Jesse chose North Carolina A & T. A few months before, in February 1960, four students from the college had made national headlines at a Woolworth's lunch counter in downtown Greensboro. They had sat down at the white-only counter

Four students demanded to be served at a Woolworth's lunch counter.

The Greensboro Sit-ins

On February 1, 1960, four black students from North Carolina Agricultural and Technical College sat down at a Woolworth's lunch counter in downtown Greensboro. The counter was for whites only. Blacks could only eat standing up. But the students refused to move until they were served.

The four students were named Joseph McNeil, Franklin McCain, David Richmond, and Ezell Blair, Jr. They started the sit-in movement because they were opposed to segregation. Tired of just talking, they wanted to do something about it.

The sit-in in Greensboro inspired other students at other colleges to protest segregation with sit-ins, boycotts, and picketing. Always, the protesters resisted using violence.

The great civil rights leader Dr. Martin Luther King, Jr., preached that violence would only end in beatings and death for blacks. He taught that nonviolent protest was the only way to show racist whites the error of their ways.

The sit-ins cost Woolworth's money. Worse, the sit-ins made the store look bad to the public. In the end, Woolworth's gave in and agreed to let black people eat at the counters. An important step in the civil rights movement had been taken.

and refused to get up. They were denied service, but they still sat, politely protesting the unfair treatment.

The activism of the sit-in protests appealed to Jesse, and he soon got involved. Through this work, he met another student who shared his interests. Her name was Jacqueline Lavinia Davis, and she was one year behind Jesse at school. The two attended church together, fell in love, and were married in 1962 at Jesse's home in Greenville.

After college, the Jacksons moved to Chicago, where Jesse began studying to be a minister at the Chicago Theological Seminary. He believed he had found his calling—to preach.

However, with all that was happening in the civil rights movement, it was difficult for Jesse to concentrate on his studies. In the spring of 1965, he watched a news story on television about a protest march in Selma, Alabama. Blacks there were trying to march from Selma to the state capital in Montgomery to protest the denial of their voting rights. But at the Edmund Pettus Bridge, white Selma policemen beat and gassed the crowd in order to stop the march.

After the violence on the bridge, Martin Luther King, Jr., the most respected leader in the civil rights movement, put out a call for all friends of the movement to come to Selma for another march. Right away, Jesse set about organizing his fellow students at the seminary, and he led a group of them down to Selma to march with King.

When he got to Selma, Jesse immediately took charge, even though he had no official role there. He gave orders to some marchers, and he even delivered a speech, although no one had asked him to. Andrew

Martin Luther King, Jr., led the march from Selma to Montgomery, Alabama.

Young, one of King's closest aides, remembered "getting a little annoyed because Jesse was giving orders…and nobody knew who he was."

But King was impressed by this young man who was so eager and ready to take charge. After Selma, King asked Jesse to work with him directly on a project he was planning for Chicago. Jesse agreed. He left the seminary and took a job with King's organization, the Southern Christian Leadership Conference, or SCLC.

Operation Breadbasket

The civil rights movement began in the South, where it concentrated its efforts on ending the worst forms of segregation. Dr. King's first struggle—in Montgomery in 1954—had been for the right to sit down on a crowded bus. The Greensboro sit-ins had been for the right to sit at a lunch counter.

In the North, King knew, segregation was not so obvious. But he also saw that racism there was just as bad. In northern cities, blacks were

Mayor Richard Daley

forced to live in filthy and dangerous ghettos because people in clean, safe white neighborhoods would not rent or sell homes to blacks.

In the summer of 1966, Jesse helped King stage a number of marches into white neighborhoods around Chicago to protest the unfair housing practices. Even though the marchers were peaceful, white residents often became angry and threw rocks and bottles. On one march, King was hit in the head by a brick.

Mayor Richard Daley became very embarrassed by all the press attention that King brought with him to Chicago. He promised that Chicago would change if King agreed to leave. King agreed and stopped the marches, but Daley did not keep his promises.

When King left Chicago, he left Jesse behind to run an SCLC organization called Operation Breadbasket. While the civil rights movement had at first focused on changing unfair laws, now King was concentrating on economic justice.

Many black people in Chicago were poor simply because white businessmen would not give them good jobs and white banks would not invest in black businesses or black neighborhoods. Operation Breadbasket was created to help correct this situation. The idea was to fight businesses that made money from blacks but never gave anything back to the community.

In organizing Operation Breadbasket, Jesse decided that his main weapon would be the boycott. In a boycott, people protest a company's actions by refusing to buy its products. Jesse asked white store owners who did business in black neighborhoods to hire more black workers and to buy some of their goods from companies owned by black people.

Ten thousand people marched in Chicago to protest segregation in the city's schools.

If a business refused, Jesse would spread the word that blacks should stop buying from that store. Many businesses agreed to do what Jesse asked right away. But others had to be picketed before they would agree.

The boycotts proved that even poor people have power. By working together, they can make a difference, even to big businesses. Operation Breadbasket forced white businesses in Chicago to start taking black people seriously. It created many jobs for blacks and helped many black companies get started. It also made a hero out of Jesse Jackson, at least in Chicago.

One white businessman came to hear Jesse preach at one of the regular Saturday meetings. He thought about the things Jesse was saying, about how unfair most businesses were. He wondered if he was doing all he could to help black people get the jobs they deserved. Later on, he met a black businessman at one of the meetings, and they worked together to run a chain of stores. He didn't do this because he was afraid of a boycott. He did it because it was right. Listening to Jesse Jackson convinced him of that.

A Tragedy in Memphis

On April 4, 1968, a terrible thing happened. Martin Luther King, Jr., was in Memphis, Tennessee, where he was preparing to lead a protest march. Jesse Jackson was with him to help organize the march. At about six o'clock, King walked out onto the balcony of the Lorraine Motel where the group was staying. Suddenly a shot rang out. King collapsed, shot in the head.

Jesse Jackson with Martin Luther King, Jr., and Ralph Abernathy on the balcony of the Lorraine Motel the day before King was shot.

Ralph Abernathy, a longtime King associate, was the first to reach King. He cradled his friend's head in his arms while they waited for the ambulance. Jesse called King's wife, Coretta, to tell her the shocking news. The doctors at the hospital did what they could, but within an hour, Martin Luther King, Jr., was dead.

When black people in Chicago heard about King's murder, they felt sad, frightened, and angry—all at the same time. Many blamed white people for King's death, and they rioted to show their rage. Black neighborhoods in Chicago were in flames, and nine people were already dead from the rioting. Mayor Daley ordered the police to shoot rioters on sight. Under King, the civil rights movement had been nonviolent, but suddenly everything had changed.

Rioters set fire to a building in Washington, D.C., following Martin Luther King, Jr.'s death.

Many cities called in the National Guard to maintain order.

Jesse knew he had to do something. He flew back to Chicago that night and went on television the next morning. Wearing the same bloody shirt in which he had left Memphis the night before, Jesse urged the rioters to stop. He pleaded with black people not to give up, not to lose hope. He promised that the civil rights movement would indeed go on.

People listened. The riots stopped. The fires died down. Then it was time to pick up the pieces.

"I Am Somebody"

After King's death, his aides were angry with Jesse Jackson. They thought Jesse should not have gone on television the morning after the shooting. They believed he should have been more dignified and stayed away from the press. They thought that Jesse Jackson was more interested in getting attention for himself than in honoring King.

Jesse flew back to Chicago after King was murdered.

Still, Ralph Abernathy, who succeeded King as head of the SCLC, tried to work with Jesse. During the Poor People's March, twenty thousand people camped out on the Washington Mall in front of Congress and the White House. This shanty town was called Resurrection City, and Abernathy named Jesse "City Manager."

The weather was very bad, however, and many of the protesters became upset. After some fights broke out, Jesse got up to preach. He urged the people to recite after him.

"I am," he began.

"I am," the crowd repeated.

"Somebody!" he yelled.

"Somebody!"

"I may be poor, but I am somebody," Jesse chanted. "I may be uneducated, but I am somebody. I may be unskilled, but I am somebody. I may be on dope. I may have lost hope. But I am somebody. I am black, beautiful, proud. I must be respected. I must be protected. I am God's child."

When Jesse returned to Chicago and Operation Breadbasket, he kept that speech, which grew into a prayer. His regular Saturday meetings always started with the crowd chanting, "I am somebody!"

It was a very powerful prayer. It told each person that he or she was important. Jesse remembered what it had felt like as a child to be treated as a nobody by white people. He knew it was important for blacks to feel good about themselves and to feel pride in being black.

Yet other civil rights leaders were still angry with Jesse Jackson. He was not humble, they said, the way a man of God should be. He liked being in the spotlight too much. Also, there were questions about the methods Jesse used to raise money, and questions about how he spent it. Some people charged that Jesse was only helping to make rich blacks richer with his boycotts.

In 1971, Jesse and Ralph Abernathy had a fight over Operation Breadbasket. Abernathy claimed that Jesse would not take orders. Operation Breadbasket was still part of the SCLC, but Jesse wanted to run things his own way.

That same year, Jesse resigned from Operation Breadbasket and started his own organization. It was called PUSH, which stood for People United to Serve Humanity. The focus of Operation Breadbasket had been economics, but PUSH turned instead to youth issues such as drug abuse and teenage pregnancy.

For the next ten years, Jesse visited hundreds of schools in poor black neighborhoods to spread his message: "Respect me. Protect me. Never neglect me. I am God's child."

PUSH

Jesse founded PUSH in 1971.

In the 1970s, many black students in poor neighborhoods suffered from drug and alcohol abuse, unwanted pregnancies, and gang violence in schools. As a result, young people were losing their chance to get an education and make a good future for themselves.

As the leader of PUSH, Jesse Jackson asked parents to take a greater interest in their children's education. He asked them to limit television viewing, set curfews, and keep track of their children's behavior.

He asked churches to get involved. He suggested they set up community projects to show young people they could make a difference. He also asked schools to set higher standards that might inspire students to succeed.

Finally, Jackson asked the students themselves to take charge of their lives. He asked them to sign contracts, promising not to take drugs and to study at least two hours each day. Jesse Jackson and PUSH made a difference to young people all across the country.

Jesse made his first run for the presidency in 1984.

Run, Jesse, Run

In 1983, Jesse Jackson decided that he was going to run as a Democrat for president of the United States in the 1984 election. Many people thought he was foolish to try. Ronald Reagan, one of the most popular presidents of all time, was running for re-election. And anyway, a black man could not possibly win a national election.

Still, Jesse ran because he thought it was the next logical step for the civil rights movement to take. The only way to get real political power, Jesse believed, was to vote. He knew that a black man's candidacy would help increase the black vote.

But Jesse did not run just as a black candidate. Instead, he reached out to all the poor and neglected people in the country. He called his

In 1988, Jesse ran for president again. His family was much more involved this time. Of his five children, two were very active in his campaign. Jesse, Jr., served as his father's campaign coordinator in the South, and Jonathon, who was only 22, campaigned in Virginia, North Carolina, and Washington, D.C. Later, Jesse, Jr., became the youngest black man ever to sit on the executive board of the Democratic National Committee.

The highlight of the campaign was the Michigan primary. The victory in Michigan showed that Jesse had indeed learned a lot about how to campaign and how to attract a wider base of support. This time, he won 6.7 million votes, 12 states, and 1,157 delegates. But he could not catch Michael Dukakis. Many people thought that Jesse's strong second-place finish had earned him the vice-presidential nomination. But Dukakis chose Senator Lloyd Bentsen of Texas instead.

Jesse's campaign excited millions of blacks, young and old alike.

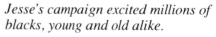

Jesse Jackson with his family at the 1988 Democratic convention.

Even though he was not given the vice-presidential nomination, Jesse Jackson had gained power in the Democratic party. He reminded Democrats that many of their members were poor and homeless, and in need of education and help. Michael Dukakis was the head of the Democratic party in 1988, but Jesse Jackson was the soul.

It had been a long, hard journey for Jesse Jackson. He started out a poor black boy without a father, and he had become one of the most famous men in America. Through the years, the support of his family and his own intelligence and skill took him far. But most important of all, Jesse Jackson had the drive and the will to succeed.

He still has that drive. "Be patient with me," Jesse Jackson says. "God is not finished with me yet."

Important Events in the Life of Jesse Jackson

1941   Jesse Jackson is born on October 8 in Greenville, South Carolina.

1959   Jesse enters the University of Illinois.

1960   Jesse transfers to North Carolina Agricultural and Technical College.

1962   Jesse marries Jacqueline Lavinia Davis.

1963   Jesse enters the Chicago Theological Seminary.

1966   Jesse and Martin Luther King, Jr., lead marches in Chicago for better housing for poor blacks.

          Jesse becomes head of Operation Breadbasket in Chicago.

1968   Martin Luther King, Jr., is assassinated.

1971   Jesse establishes PUSH (People United to Serve Humanity).

1983–4   Jesse runs for the Democratic party nomination for president of the United States.

1987–8   Jesse makes his second bid for the Democratic party's nomination for president. He wins the Michigan primary and comes in second behind Michael Dukakis.

Find Out More About Jesse Jackson

Books: *Jesse Jackson: A Black Leader* by Patricia Martin (Vero Beach, Fla.: Rourke, 1987).

Jesse Jackson: Keep Hope Alive by Patricia McKissack (New York: Scholastic Books, 1989).

The Picture Life of Jesse Jackson by Warren Halliburton (New York: Franklin Watts, 1984).

Videos: "Eyes on the Prize" is a documentary series that covers the whole civil rights movement.

Places: The Civil Rights Memorial in Montgomery, Alabama, is a tribute to all who participated in the struggle for civil rights. It is located at the corner of Washington and Hull Streets.

Jesse and Jacqueline celebrate with supporters at the 1988 convention.

Index